C000243356

A fascinating mixture of natural and man-made features, the broads were created in part through the silting up of the river mouths which caused the streams to flow more slowly and widen out into shallow meres. The digging of peat for fuel also played a part in the process. For many hundreds of years considerable quantities of peat were taken from the area until, some five or six hundred years ago, the abandoned diggings began to flood, creating the reed-fringed lakes we see today. Thronged with sailing boats, rowing dinghies and motor cruisers for much of the year, they are now protected by the Broads Authority set up in 1989. Controlling one hundred and thirty miles of waterways, it aims to monitor and balance the competing demands of human activities such as boating and tourism with the needs of conservation and wildlife. The Norfolk and Suffolk Broads constitute the largest protected wetland area in Britain, and the third largest inland waterway. Here it is possible to find both bustling yachting centres such as **Oulton Broad** (*middle*) with its boat yards and hire facilities, and more peaceful scenes such as rural **Salhouse Broad** (*top*). At **Ranworth Broad** (*right*) rowing-boats lie on their moorings in a tranquil backwater. The result of centuries of interaction between people and their environment, the Norfolk Broads has similar status to the National Parks. Although perhaps best known as a sailing and boating centre, the Broads also have several important wildlife reserves and nature trails.

Although there have been immense changes
in the landscape of East Anglia in the last
fifty years, Norfolk still offers some of the
most significant wildlife habitats in Britain.
Nature conservation has long held a vital
place in the county for it was here that the
first of the County Naturalists' Trusts, now
The Norfolk Wildlife Trust, was formed in
1926, and many of Norfolk's nature
reserves are important national sites.

Kingfishers, coots and swans are familiar
sights on rivers and lakes across the
region. The **coot** (*above*) is the largest
member of the rail family, distinguished
from the moorhen by the conspicuous
white patch on its forehead. A poor flyer,
it prefers to run from danger or paddle
across the surface of the water on its
partially webbed feet. The coot's nest is a
substantial floating platform which is
anchored among vegetation in shallow
water. **Mute swans** (*top left*) are Britain's
only resident species of swan and can
weigh up to 40 lb. Distinguished from
other species by their orange bills and
gracefully curved necks, they frequent
lakes and ponds, slow-flowing rivers and
wetlands beside salt or brackish water.
The pretty little **bearded tit** (*left*) is
mainly confined to East Anglia and
neighbouring parts of the east coast
where it is found in the beds of reed,
mace and sedge which grow alongside
rivers and meres. It builds its nest of
sedges lined with fine grass only a few
inches above water-level and its principal
food is insects and water snails. The last
remaining haunt of the **swallowtail
butterfly** (*bottom*) is in the fens
surrounding the Norfolk Broads. The
largest and one of the most beautiful of
British butterflies, it has a three-inch
wingspan and a strong, flapping flight. It
is seen in May and June.

Norfolk Broads

A unique blend of river, mere and windmill, the Norfolk Broads attract visitors in their hundreds of thousands. There are nearly 200 miles of waterways to explore, studded with bustling riverside boating centres. The main rivers connect a network of broads, open areas of water which are thought to be ancient peat diggings created by man, ideal for sailing and motor cruisers. When the people have left, however, the Broads still offer a fascinating and beautiful landscape where the open sky, distant horizons, reed beds and village 'staithes' have for centuries provided inspiration for artists. The area is also a naturalist's paradise, being home to a wide variety of wildlife. Some of the rarest birds in the country are found here and endangered species like the swallowtail butterfly flourish.

Norfolk Broads

Windmills have been a characteristic feature of the low-lying East Anglian landscape since medieval times. While some have been used for grinding corn to make flour, many others served as drainage pumps, using the power of the wind to turn scoop wheels removing surplus water off the land. These have now been largely replaced by electric pumps. Some of the many Broadland mills, like **Turf Fen Mill** (*left*), have been successfully restored, others have been converted into homes or allowed to become picturesque ruins. The landscape of the Norfolk Broads is made up of a network of meandering rivers, dykes and open expanses of water comprising twelve large and twenty-four small lakes or meres. The most important Broadland rivers are the Bure, the Yare and the Waveney. With their principal tributaries, the Ant and the Thurne, they provide nearly two hundred miles of waterways.

Also known as a dabchick, the **little grebe** (*above*) is a common sight on inland waters and estuaries throughout Britain. Its nest is little more than a raft of floating weeds and reeds, usually near the edge of the water. Diving when disturbed to surface some distance away, this tailless little bird can be seen on lakes and rivers in the Broads wherever there is plenty of vegetation. One of the most endangered birds in Britain, the **bittern** (*below left*) lost most of its nesting sites when the marshes were drained, and had ceased to breed in Britain by the mid-19th century. This shy and semi-nocturnal bird is now re-established in a number of areas, notably the reed beds around Hickling and Horsey where its brown

plumage, striped with black, affords it good camouflage. The **mallard** (*below right*) is the most numerous and widespread of our wild ducks. The drake is also one of the most attractive with its velvety green head, white collar and vivid blue wing feathers. In addition to our resident birds, Norfolk attracts many migrating species which make landfall here.

River Bure

The most northerly of the three main Broadland rivers, the Bure was once navigable from its junction with the River Yare in Great Yarmouth as far as Aylsham; now the last nine miles beyond Coltishall is closed to boats. **Aylsham** (*right*) is a bustling market town which was first recorded in the Domesday survey in 1085. The Market Place is surrounded by some fine old buildings including the Black Boy Inn, once a stopping place for the Cromer to Norwich stagecoach. The famous landscape gardener Humphry Repton is buried in the churchyard.

Impressive **Buxton Watermill** (*left*) stands midway between Aylsham and Coltishall. Here the River Bure falls several feet, generating a considerable amount of power, and a mill is known to have stood on this site since at least the 11th century. The present building, which is Grade II listed, dates from 1754, although it was largely rebuilt to the original design in the 1990s after a disastrous fire. Buxton is one of the stops on the **Bure Valley Railway** (*bottom left*) which runs for nine miles through beautiful Broadland scenery, linking Aylsham and Wroxham. Opened in 1990, it is the longest miniature railway to be built in Britain since the 1920s and operates over a section of the old Great Eastern line. Planned as an integral part of the project, the Bure Valley Walk and Cycle Path was constructed alongside the track of the railway.

Hoveton Hall Gardens (*right*), in the Broadland village of Hoveton St. John on the River Bure, is a delightful 15-acre garden consisting of a mixture of formal and informal planting. A picturesque gardener's cottage stands in one corner of the formal walled garden which was laid out in the 1930s and is known as the Spider Garden because of the intriguing design of the iron gate which leads into it.

Not far from Hoveton is the attractive village of **Belaugh** (*left*) where the staithe provides moorings for a few pleasure craft. The church is a prominent landmark, situated on a mound above a wide bend in the river. The head of navigation on the Bure, **Coltishall** (*bottom*) is a popular port of call for small-boat enthusiasts. There are some fine Georgian houses in the village which also boasts two riverside pubs full of Broadland atmosphere.

Wroxham (*top* and *bottom*) was the first of the Broadland villages to cater for holiday-makers when a boat yard began to hire out yachts towards the end of the 19th century. It is now one of the principal boating centres on the Broads, providing for all the needs of holiday-makers including boat-hire, shops and hotels.

Wroxham Broad (*middle*) is formed out of the River Bure and here the Norfolk Broads Yacht Club is based and regattas are held. The fine old bridge, which was built in 1614 and later widened, joins Wroxham with its twin village of Hoveton and offers delightful views of the River Bure as it winds through some of the most charming countryside in Norfolk.

With its shops and cottages grouped around the green beside the staithe and its three riverside inns, **Horning** (*right*) is one of the prettiest and most popular ports of call for river goers on the Broads. Standing downstream from the staithe is weatherboarded little **Horning Mill** (*below*) which has been converted to provide living accommodation on the ground floor.

The ancient river crossing at **Horning Ferry** (*left*) has been in use for over 1,000 years. The present Ferry Inn, a popular port of call for yachtsmen, replaced the original thatched inn which was destroyed by a bomb which fell during the Second World War.

The charming village of **Woodbastwick** (*left*) lies just south of the River Bure. It has one of the most photogenic village greens in the county, surrounded by 19th century estate cottages, many of them thatched and some with Biblical texts on their frontages. A thatched well-house stands on the green and nearby is the Church of St. Fabian and St. Sebastian, also thatched, which is the only church in the country to be dedicated jointly to these two saints. Sir Giles Gilbert Scott was responsible for restoring the church which contains some colourful stained glass and interesting monuments. Situated between Cockshoot and Salhouse Broads, the village is surrounded by reed beds and woodland which provide an ideal environment for a wide variety of birds including marsh harriers, warblers and bearded tits. Set amidst trees, **Salhouse Broad** (*right*) is one of the loveliest of the broads. Accessible on foot as well as by boat or car, it is popular not only with sailors but with walkers, picnickers and bird-watchers. The broad covers an area of some 32 acres, surrounded by sedge and reed beds, grassland and

woodland which combine to attract a wide variety of wildfowl, herons and other wildlife. Created among the woods of oak and alder that surround South Walsham Inner Broad, the **Fairhaven Woodland and Water Garden** (*below*) is a paradise for wildlife. Cultivated organically, the gardens are known especially for their water-loving plants, flowering shrubs and year-round interest.

Erosion of the soft banks of the River Bure has brought the foundations of **St. Benet's Abbey** (*right*), once a wealthy Benedictine monastery, right to the edge of the river. The only abbey in Norfolk before the Norman Conquest, St. Benet's was also the only religious house not closed down by Henry VIII during the Dissolution of the Monasteries. It passed to the Bishop of Norwich who, in his role as Abbot, still holds an outdoor service here each August. In the 18th century a local farmer built a windpump on the site. The top was blown off in a gale in 1863, but the massive cone, still standing in the abbey gatehouse, is one of the Broads' more unusual sights. The drainage mill known as **St. Benet's Level Mill** (*right*) stands a short distance away between the River Bure and the River Thurne. This splendid tower mill dates from the late 18th century and was used to move water from drainage ditches back into the main river.

South Walsham Broad (*left*) has one of the most picturesque settings on the Broads, and consists of two stretches of water linked to the Bure by the meandering Fleet Dyke. The staithe looks out across the tree-rimmed waters of the outer broad which is always busy with yachts and other small boats. The inner broad, a haven for wildlife, is privately owned by The Fairhaven Garden Trust.

The largest broad in the Bure valley, **Ranworth** is divided into two parts. Inner Broad, which is privately owned, provides a peaceful haven for wildfowl. The other, known as **Malthouse Broad** (*right*), is much frequented by pleasure boats. There are panoramic views of Ranworth Broad and of the wide Bure Valley from the tower of **St. Helen's Parish Church** (*below*). Known as the 'Cathedral of the Broads', Ranworth Church contains what is probably the finest painted medieval rood-screen in the country as well as some outstanding carvings and a remarkable fifteenth-century illuminated songbook, known as the *Ranworth Antiphoner*.

Ranworth Staithe (*bottom*), with its moorings and attractive green, is a popular port of call. A short walk away, the Broadland Conservation Centre houses an exhibition on the ecology and wildlife of the Broads. Incorporating a viewing gallery, the floating centre is thatched with local reeds and is imaginatively situated on a pontoon at the edge of Ranworth Broad.

A busy destination for boating enthusiasts, **Acle Bridge** (*top*) has two boat yards offering boat hire as well as good moorings, a riverside inn and fine views along the River Bure. The Acle Sailing Regatta, which takes place to the west of the bridge, attracts yachtsmen from all across the Broads. Gateway to the Broads, the village of **Acle** (*bottom*) lies about a mile from the river on the main road from Norwich to Great Yarmouth. It has some

very attractive 17th and 18th century buildings and an ancient thatched church which is known to date in part from Saxon times, although the eight-sided belfry was modified in the 1400s. North of Acle the River Bure meets the River Thurne at **Thurne Mouth** (*above*). This is a particularly popular area with yachtsmen because, unlike many places on the Broads, the water is open and not overhung with trees. The Thurne Mouth Regatta is a regular fixture on the sailing calendar.

On the northern bank of the River Bure about a mile below Acle, **Stokesby** (*above*) is a delightful village with a wide, tree-lined green and a riverside inn which is a popular stopping place for boats travelling to or from Yarmouth. Alongside the green is the public staithe where boats can

find safe moorings. A short distance below Stokesby is **Stracey Arms** (*bottom*) where a fine drainage mill stands beside the water. Situated where the River Bure meets the River Yare, **Great Yarmouth Yacht Station** (*left*) is always busy with leisure craft. Operated by the Broads Authority, it provides safe moorings but must be approached at the right state of the tide because of low bridges in the area.

Great Yarmouth has for
centuries been an important
centre of the fishing industry,
known especially for its
herrings. There is still a busy
commercial harbour (*bottom*)
providing safe anchorage for a
variety of coastal vessels. Boat
trips along the River Yare and
the Broads start from the town
and on Marine Parade (*right*)
the Maritime Museum contains
exhibitions relating to the
maritime history of East Anglia
including the fisheries, life-
saving and shipbuilding. With
the arrival of the railway in the
19th century, came the tourists
and a whole new leisure
industry. Great Yarmouth now
has two piers, attractive parks
and gardens and the large
Marina Centre. Four miles of
sandy beaches offer a variety
of traditional seaside
entertainments and at night the
front becomes a blaze of lights.

River Ant

A tributary of the River Bure, and the smallest of the three northern rivers, the River Ant flows through some of the most enchanting scenery in Broadland. **Ludham Bridge** (*right* and *centre*), the first port of call after leaving the Bure, is thronged with all types of craft for much of the year. Surrounded by fields, marshes and a network of rivers, the village of Ludham is a delightful place of thatched cottages, inns and a notable 15th century church. Beautiful **How Hill** (*bottom*) near Ludham provides one of the most peaceful and traditional scenes in Broadland. Overlooked by graceful Turf Fen Mill, the River Ant winds between reed marshes which provide a habitat for water-loving birds such as the hen harrier, the bittern, the bearded tit and the reed warbler. An Environmental Centre has been set up here by the Broads Authority to enable people to observe the wide variety of birds without disturbing them. The reed beds are still harvested, although not on the scale on which they once produced quantities of Norfolk reed for use in thatching.

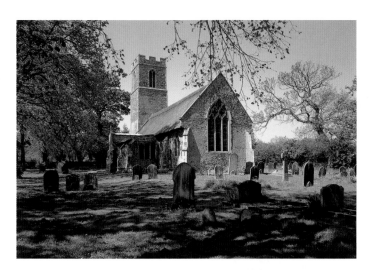

Between Ludham Bridge and Barton Broad the River Ant winds between wooded banks and meadows on one of the prettiest stretches of the river. Just south of Barton Broad is the quiet village of **Irstead**. St. Michael's Church (*left*), with its thatched roof and sturdy tower, contains a number of noteworthy items including a 14th century font, a linenfold panelled pulpit, carved bench ends and some interesting 14th century ironwork on the door.

To the west of Barton Broad a dyke leads to **Neatishead** (*right*), a remote little village which lies at the head of a wooded creek. Surrounded by delightful walks, the staithe provides moorings for small boats. A small channel leads from Barton Broad to the village of **Barton Turf** (*below*) where there is a boat yard and a shop catering for the needs of those who are travelling by water.

As it meanders through some of the most picturesque and unspoilt scenery in the Norfolk Broads, the River Ant passes a number of fine old mills, among them **Hunsett Mill** (*left*). This old drainage mill stands in isolation between Sutton Broad and Wayford Bridge not far from the small market town of Stalham. A lane leads from the town to **Stalham Staithe** (*below*) with its excellent moorings.

Situated on the upper reaches of the Ant near the limit of navigation, **Wayford Bridge** (*below*) is an ancient crossing point taking the road over the river. The staithe offers several moorings and provides a convenient stopping place for boats which need to lower their canopy before heading under the bridge where, at high water, the headroom is only seven feet. From the bridge there are good views of this picturesque stretch of the river.

River Thurne

A wide river, although it is only six miles long, the Thurne flows through some of the most open country in the Norfolk Broads. An ideal stretch of water for sailing and boating activities, it is always busy with yachts and other small boats. **Thurne Dyke** (*below*) leads to the village of Thurne with its convenient moorings and other facilities for the boats which use this popular part of the river.

White-painted, **Thurne Mill** (*top*) stands at the entrance to the short dyke. This well-known landmark, which can be seen for miles, is a popular subject for photographers. Originally built for drainage, it was badly damaged by a gale in 1919. Now owned by The Norfolk Windmills Trust, it has been successfully restored and is open to the public. It can occasionally be seen working.

Womack Water (*right*) is a narrow waterway which branches off the River Thurne about a mile from Ludham. It extends north-westwards for nearly a mile, and at the far end, where trees overhang the water, a staithe provides delightful moorings.

Conveniently situated on the north bank of the River Thurne, **Potter Heigham** (*top left* and *bottom*) is a popular centre for touring on the Norfolk Broads. Hotels, shops and boat yards are all gathered around the famous medieval bridge which is more than seven hundred years old. The central arch is so low that many boats have to wait for low tide to pass safely beneath it. About two miles from the coast is the attractive village of **West Somerton**, known as the birthplace of Robert Hales, the 'Norfolk Giant'. Born in 1820, he grew to a height of 7 feet 8 inches and was once presented to Queen Victoria. West Somerton Staithe (*centre left*) lies close to the coast road and footpaths lead inland from the village to Martham Broad which is also sometimes known as Somerton Broad. This peaceful spot on the River Thurne is managed by The Norfolk Naturalists' Trust and is an important breeding ground for birds such as the bittern and the harrier.

Owned by The National Trust along with Horsey Mere and more than 2,000 acres of the surrounding countryside, **Horsey Mill** (*above*) was originally built to help drain the marshes by pumping water from the dykes into the river. This fine tower mill continued to work until 1943 when it was severely damaged by lightning. It has now been restored and is one of the largest mills remaining on the Broads. The Mere is a favourite place for sailing – a Site of Special Scientific Interest and one of the largest areas of open water in the Broads. The largest of all the broads, **Hickling Broad** is a vast, shallow expanse of water, fringed with reeds. Because it is so shallow it is necessary for sailing boats to keep to a marked channel to avoid the danger of running aground. At the head of the broad is Hickling Staithe (*bottom*) with its moorings, boat yards and picturesque waterside inn. This area is almost as popular with fishermen and bird-watchers as with small-boat enthusiasts. The marshlands around Hickling are an important habitat for birds with bitterns, harriers, bearded tits and the occasional osprey among the resident population, while migrating birds also make landfall here.

River Yare

Longest of the Broadland rivers, the River Yare extends over fifty-five miles from its source near East Dereham through Norwich to the sea. On its way it flows through a number of attractive villages. At **Reedham** (*right*) the river is crossed by a chain ferry, the only river crossing point for cars downstream of Norwich. With its riverside green and Ferry Inn, Reedham makes a pleasant stopping place for holiday-makers on the river.

At one time the River Chet, a tributary of the Yare, was busy with wherries carrying goods from **Loddon Mill** (*left*), but as the trade lessened the river became overgrown and shallow. Now it has been opened up again and yachts are able to sail up to the little town of Loddon with its excellent moorings and other facilities. The vast tidal expanse of **Breydon Water** (*below*) stretches for over three miles from Burgh Castle, where it is entered by the Rivers Yare and Waveney, up to Great Yarmouth. The surrounding area is the largest protected wetland in the United Kingdom, an important haven for both resident and over-wintering birds. At low tide, the mud-flats are covered by wading birds and wildfowl and a thriving colony of common tern has been established on artificial islands.

Once **Rockland Staithe**
(*below*) was a busy wharf and
port of call for the wherries
which transported the black-
glazed roof tiles down the
River Yare from Rockland
where they were made. A
reminder of those times, the
long-distance footpath known
as Wherryman's Way winds
past this peaceful Broadland
hamlet. Two miles from
Rockland, surrounded by
open country, is the busy
boating centre of **Brundall**
(*left*) with its boat yards,
marina and local sailing club.

Norwich

Norwich is a medieval city of great beauty which was once surrounded by a four-mile-long city wall, sections of which can still be seen. Its long and varied history is reflected in its many interesting old buildings and quaint corners. Picturesque, flint-cobbled **Elm Hill** (*right*), in the old quarter, is lined with charming timber-framed and colour-washed houses, many of them dating from Tudor or Georgian times, and is preserved much as it would have looked 400 years ago. **Norwich Cathedral** (*below right*) is considered to be one of the finest ecclesiastical buildings in the country. The foundation stone of this impressive structure was laid in 1096 and it is particularly known for its extensive cloisters and its fine array of flying buttresses. The lofty tower with its slender spire rises to 315 feet and, among English cathedrals, is second only to Salisbury in height. The nave roof is decorated with a splendid series of bosses which tell the story of mankind from the Creation to the Last Judgment. The tree-lined yacht station is situated on the River Wensum in the heart of the city, only a few minutes' walk away from the cathedral. It provides moorings and other facilites for visitors arriving in the city by boat or starting out from here to explore the Norfolk Broads.

The ancient gateway known as **Pull's Ferry** (*above*) takes its name from an 18th century ferryman who plied across the River Wensum, and the old ferryman's house still stands next to an ancient flint water-gate. Much of the beautiful white stone used to build Norwich cathedral was brought from Caen in Normandy, and in the 15th century the water-gate guarded a little canal, built by the monks, through which the stone was transported at the end of its long journey from France. Today it is one of the most frequently photographed and most picturesque spots in the city. The Normans were responsible for building both the cathedral and the castle. **Norwich Castle** (*below*) is an impressive stone motte and bailey structure with an ornate keep which is prominently situated on the highest point of the town. It was originally built as a royal palace, and in 1121 King Henry I spent Christmas here with his court. The strategic military importance of the castle diminished in medieval times after a four-mile-long wall was built around the city. Used for more than five hundred years as a county gaol, it was greatly restored in Victorian times and now houses a museum and a world-famous collection of paintings by artists of the 'Norwich School', including John Crome (1768-1821) and John Cotman (1782-1842).

River Waveney

For nearly the whole of its length the Waveney forms the border between Norfolk and Suffolk. Situated at its junction with the River Yare, **Burgh Castle** (*right*) is one of a chain of castles built by the Romans to defend the east coast against Saxon invaders. Sections of the massive walls still stand, and from here there are good views across the surrounding marshland. Further along the river is the village of **St. Olaves** (*below*), site of a ruined Augustinian priory. First mention of a bridge over the river at this point was in 1296, but no permanent structure was completed until the 18th century. The current suspension bridge is the first bridging point on the River Waveney above Great Yarmouth.

Situated within reach of both Norwich and the coast, as well as the beautiful Yare and Waveney valleys, **Burgh Castle Marina** (*below*) attracts not only yachtsmen, but also holiday-makers, fishing enthusiasts and bird-watchers. With its pontoon moorings, slipway and boat building services it provides welcome facilities for small-boat enthusiasts.

Fed by the River Waveney, **Oulton Broad** (*above* and *below right*) is the most southerly of the Broads, connected to Lowestoft by a lake. This popular yachting centre, with its moorings, boat yards and hire facilities, is always busy with pleasure craft, especially in the summer months when regattas and a water carnival are added attractions.

Somerleyton Hall (*below*) is a splendid Victorian mansion built in the Anglo-Italian style as a tangible sign of the prosperity of the new Victorian aristocracy. Built around the shell of an earlier Tudor and Jacobean house, it has extravagent architectural features, magnificent carved stonework and some impressive staterooms which contain fine paintings and carvings. In the gardens, little changed since Victorian times; there are abundant flowering trees and shrubs, statuary and a remarkable yew maze.

Once a broad tidal estuary where wherries and barges traded, the River Waveney is now used mainly by pleasure craft and, as the river widens out near the largely Georgian town of **Beccles**, it provides good opportunities for sailing. The centre of the town is a conservation area containing many buildings of historic interest. One of the most prominent features in Beccles is the 97-foot-high bell tower of St. Michael's Parish Church which stands slightly apart from the main body of the church. St. Michael's, which dates from about 1370, stands in a commanding position overlooking the valley, and from the church there are delightful views of the river as it winds through the town and the surrounding countryside. The quay is a bustling centre of activity, especially in the summer months when visitors to the Broads make full use of the moorings. The Beccles Sailing Club, one of the oldest clubs on the Broads, founded in 1907, also holds an annual regatta here. From the town there is a signposted walk along the river and over the marshes called the Marsh Trail. It provides walkers with excellent opportunities to observe the plants and wildlife which inhabit the area as well as to enjoy some superb Broadland scenery.